First English Edition
ISBN: 978-1-7372780-2-3
Library of Congress Control Number: 2022942202
Written by Maytê Carvalho
Translated by Ashley Adams, Fatima Carvalho, Lindsey Howard, Maria Claudia Paroni, Rafael Rocca
Copy Editing by Ana Silvani & Maria Acero
Cover Art by Drica Lobo
Cover Design by Natalia Ordaz
Formatting by Ana Silvani
Manufactured in the United States of America

Let's Publish Together!

ENGLISH EDITION BY

WEBOOK PUBLISHING

MAYTÊ CARVALHO

PERSUASION

HOW TO PITCH

YOUR IDEAS

AND OWN THE ROOM

PERSUASION

To Bruno, Claudio, Fatima, Ian, and Paula, with love

PERSUASION

NOTICE

*The following pages contain truths.
If you are not prepared to know if you have been
manipulated your whole life, stop here.
Every speech hides invisible dynamics of power
and influence.*

PERSUASION

PERSUASION

With great power comes great responsibility

Ben Parker
Peter Parker's Uncle, Spider-Man

CONTENTS

AUTHOR'S NOTE

I see this book, which at first seemed to me much more about personal and individual development, as more of a tool for social change and as a critical and reflective interpretation of this moment in which we live.

We are persuaded by the press, by politicians, and by propaganda every day, so we need to be alert and watch out not to be manipulated.

At the end of this book, I would like us to be able to exercise this critical view while reading a newspaper, seeing a news item, or while watching an advertisement on television. And then reflect: What is this? Is this teasing me? Is this seducing me? Why is it using that specific word? What is the political agenda of the sender of this message?

The reading of the world must precede the reading of the word; that is why an education that helps people to analyze realities is extremely necessary. Language and reality are dynamically related. The understanding of a text achieved by critical reading implies the perception of a relationship between text and context.

When we read the world, we expand our human condition: we reach higher spheres and perceive dynamics that were previously invisible. This ability makes us active subjects with the ability to create and recreate our lives: political, social, and individual.

Understanding this dynamic allows you to take control of your life because there are invisible subtleties of power and influence in our every speech and relationship. When we manage to give a name and a surname to these dynamics, it is possible to better understand our being in the world. We begin to understand how to better conduct our relationships in order to succeed and exercise the full power of being who we truly are. I hope this book leads to shifting your view of self, as you are the protagonist in your own life, and creates an active voice for you in your relationships, at work, and in your life.

In a world with undefined contours in relation to the spirit of time and the *modus operandi* that awaits us, all I can do is propose that we go together in this crossing. And may this book be part of that journey, opening our eyes and ears to the invisible.

Maytê Carvalho
Los Angeles, California
June 2022

PERSUASION

PERSUASION

FOREWORD

By Shelley Zalis

Shelley Zalis is the CEO of The Female Quotient. Known as the "chief troublemaker," she's a pioneer for online market research and advancing women in workplace.

A Highlight of my year was reading *PERSUASION: How To Pitch Your Ideas And Own The Room.*

It's a treasure trove of knowledge that provides insight into navigating the business world while helping women find and amplify their voices. This book is a powerful reminder that we are in control of our lives and careers – a must read for any ambitious person.

Los Angeles, July 2022

PERSUASION

INTRODUCTION

The invisible dynamics of influence on persuasive speech

Since I began teaching persuasion and rhetoric in extension courses at the Escola Superior de Propaganda e Marketing (ESPM – School of Advertising & Marketing) in São Paulo, many people have asked me: "why don't you write a book on persuasion?"

I postponed it for as long as possible because, in a way, I thought: could my classes result in a book? And I just felt safe enough to do so after having taught my course to over a thousand people and having received so much wonderful feedback from my students – who earned more in their professional work, made the revenue of their businesses grow, and even changed the way they communicated with friends, improving their personal relationships.

Every text message, call, and feedback in class gave me a sense of mission: I needed to spread this content to as many people as possible! I wanted to affect the lives of everyone who wakes up determined to take the reins of their own life but feels the need to be better equipped to do so.

I have always been an enthusiast of therapy (I do psychoanalysis) and, therefore, I see the movement of narrating one's own story as a therapeutic act. How we express ourselves, the words we choose, how we approach the people around us, reveal patterns and dynamics that are often invisible.

When we learn about fallacies, discourses, and ways of constructing a narrative, we learn mainly how to preserve ourselves from the abuse of others and to question the health of our relationships. What you will learn in this book can be used for good or for bad – I hate Manichaeism, but somehow thinking of the Western construct of bad/good, this statement makes sense. When we become aware of attitudes that were previously replicated, it is necessary to own our responsibility as an individual within a dynamic world.

No matter what your job is, much of your success will depend on your ability to influence and persuade others. In other words, get them to say yes to your requests, be it negotiating with suppliers, selling your product to buyers, leading employees, or asking the boss for a raise. Persuading is necessary for our success in professional life.

Far beyond the professional, the effects can also be felt in our personal life. The way we conduct (or are conducted by) our relationships, whether they are intimate, friendly, or familial, can show signs of abusive or healthy dynamics.

The whole idea for this book came about because when I was 18, I participated in a television show called *The Apprentice*. I won the *The Apprentice Special Edition*, and then I participated in the *University Apprentice – The Return*, from which I was eliminated. Right after, I started my career in Advertising.

After working in the WPP advertising group, I decided to venture alone. I founded some companies and owned a cosmetics app, which led me to pitch on the Shark Tank Brazil program and get an angel investor. We will talk about pitch, which is persuasive speech, later in this book.

After becoming an entrepreneur, I began working in the investment fund of that start-up, and then moved to Los Angeles, California, where I took the position of Business strategy director at one of the largest advertising agencies in the world, TBWA Chiat Day whose main clients include Apple, McDonald's, and Disney. Right now, I'm currently NY based, and I serve as Chief Strategy Officer of CUBO NY, an ad agency whose main clients include Pepsico, Unilever and Spotify. I bring to this book both my academic experience, and mostly, my corporate and entrepreneurial learnings.

I suggest that you read this book linearly because I follow a rationale from the introduction to talking about the fundamentals of persuasion and segmenting it in order to give you the basic repertoire so that you can later learn the praxis.

So, if you want to go straight to the chapter "How to write persuasive emails," you will notice that I am going to make some references to ethos, pathos, and logos, the content of one of the first chapters in the book.

I reinforce my suggestion: read the book in chronological and linear order because you will have more substance to follow the reading later when we are in the more practical chapters.

I would very much like that at the end of the book, you can achieve four things:

1. Develop a persuasive strategic speech (sales pitch, investment, or general presentation);

2. Present storytelling in a tactical way with a theoretical basis (Aristotle);

3. Succeed in counter-arguing, defending your ideas, projects and points of view in meetings, debates, discussions with your significant other, and controversial talks at Christmas dinner with your relatives (lol);

4. Exercise a critical and reflective point of view in order to know whether or not you are being manipulated by a persuasive narrative (whether by the media, at work, in relationships).

When you realize you're bigger than the place
where people put you in,
get out!

1-ARISTOTELIAN RHETORIC AND THE CURRENT WORLD

All my life I have heard that I am a very persuasive person. Since I was a child, my friends would say: "Maytê, go ask the teacher for this. You are the boldest." Or yet: "You're going to ask your mother for me to sleep at your house. You can convince her." My friends from my school would not let me lie: I was a class representative & class valedictorian.

I grew up with it, and in a way, I had difficulty accepting myself because I thought: "If everyone knows I'm persuasive, no one will trust what I say. People will see me as a kind of imposter."

And I felt like an imposter. I believed that this was a gift, but at the same time, I believed that I could not appropriate myself of this skill because people could say: "watch out for her: she is very persuasive," and I did not want to become that person.

After *The Apprentice*, the tv host always emphasized how persuasive I was in every meeting - and how powerful my rhetoric was - I realized that, since the entirety of Brazil knew I was persuasive, there was no longer any way to pretend otherwise. So, I decided to take this on by studying Rhetoric as an art and science.

I found out that a pejorative view of a person being persuasive is a very recent construct. In the past, it was seen as a virtue.

In 5th century BC, when Classical Greece was still Macedonia, people had classes in rhetoric and persuasion. Since childhood, they learned mathematics, philosophy, and Rhetoric. So much so that Aristotle is considered the father of rhetoric as he produced his works at that time.

I recommend Aristotle's book *Rhetoric*: it changed my life. Aristotle created Rhetoric as we know it today.

"In Aristotelian Rhetoric, we find knowledge as theory, knowledge as art, and knowledge as science. Theoretical knowledge and technical knowledge, artistic knowledge, and scientific knowledge. In the transition from the old to the new rhetoric, it naturally transformed itself from the art of persuasive communication into the hermeneutic science of interpretation."

Imagine Aristotle, back in 5th century BC in Macedonia, philosophizing with his students. Philosophers back then shared their knowledge with everyone, and it must have been hard to be a philosopher then. Especially when we talk about pay.

Aristotle needed to do some *freelance jobs* to pay the bills, let us put it that way! I mean, let us say he worked as a freelance mentor. And he took a job to coach the son of a Macedonian king: the boy Alexander, who when he became an adult years later, became known as Alexander the Great.

So, imagine yourself together with them, watching this gathering taking place between Aristotle and Alexander the Great. Alexander had an army that lacked efficiency compared to the army of his adversary, Darius. War at that time (nowadays too, but mainly then) had a very territorial purpose. They badly needed to conquer territories so that they could obtain hegemony. But how are you going to do that if you do not have a decent army?

By decent army, I mean good horses, good weapons, strong and prepared soldiers.

Alexander had none of these, but even so, he never lost a battle. He had the power of rhetoric and the people. And with Aristotle as a teacher, Alexander managed to engage and mobilize his army through his speeches. Speaking well was as important to the king as the hero is to fighting well.

He knew each soldier by name and each man's history. He teased, seduced, or intimidated according to what he knew worked with each member of his army. The result was a highly motivated and engaged team.

Making a parallel with the current world, it looks a lot like teams in the job market, doesn't it?

When looking at a competitor company – if you are the founder of a company or if you sometimes work on a project with a team – you say: "My God, the competition!

That guy went to Harvard, has several offices, and I... I look like the Brancaleone's army."

However, if you know how to engage and motivate your team members, you can go further, achieve goals, and surpass results.

There is a film by the director Oliver Stone that tells the story of Alexander the Great. Titled *Alexander*, the film shows how he influenced the minds of each soldier by calling them by name, evoking revenge on the part of their families. And that army, even though it was smaller, even though it was weaker, they never lost a war. It is worth watching. His speech evokes the "us *versus* them."

"Us *vs.* them" is a narrative widely used in the contemporary world, despite being very old. Strengthening the "we" entity creates a feeling of communion against the opposing team. It could be in Macedonia, between Darius and Alexander the Great, but if I am talking about a commercial environment, it could be "we Company X" *versus* "we Company Y".

Both discourses evoke ethos, pathos, and logos, which are the three fundamental pillars of the construction of a rhetoric discourse capable of convincing anyone. We will explore these pillars in the next chapter.

I found out that a pejorative view of a person being persuasive is a very recent construct. In the past, it was seen as a virtue.

PERSUASION

2- WHO ARE YOU, HOW DO YOU MAKE ME FEEL, AND HOW DO YOU PROVE TO ME WHAT YOU SAY?

EPL: Ethos, Pathos, Logos

Every persuasive narrative has three pillars: ethos, pathos, and logos.

What are these three pillars? Whether in a sales pitch for a start-up or in a presentation with a company, we have to make sure that we are covering a checklist called EPL (Ethos + Pathos + Logos).

Ethos is one of the most important aspects we can observe in a discourse or a narrative as it concerns the character of the speaker. Ethos is credibility: "Why should I believe in you? What have you done in your life that proves to me that you are a competent, capable person, or that you understand this subject?"

Therefore, it is your personal background and your reputation that is the most important of the three pillars. A speech can have pathos and logos, which are passion and reason, but if you do not have confidence and credibility (ethos), you could provide the audience with data that will not agree with your truth.

While logos sells reason, pathos evokes our emotions. They are antagonistic. Pathos works with empathy and vulnerability; it makes you emotional. Do you remember that political speech or that sales pitch that makes you want to cry at the end? It is a pathos-oriented speech.

Ethos	**Pathos**	**Logos**
CREDIBILITY	EMOTION	LOGIC

On the other hand, logos will give you logical proof that what is being said is true: surveys, sources, graphical data, and numbers. Everything that orbits in the sphere of the reason is logos.

It is very difficult for us to build a discourse that does not go through these three pillars. Therefore, Aristotle says we must cover these three aspects. Without saying, some speeches will be more pathos-oriented, others more logos-oriented, but in general you need to cover all three to be successful in your persuasive narrative.

ETHOS

Have you ever heard a speech in which people talk a lot about themselves? What they did professionally, the companies they have sold, the places they have worked, the academic information they have? In a way, they are talking about their personal lives. However, there is no way to isolate the credibility of who you are from your speech.

You will pitch in your start-up, for example. I often already know who you are. I have your personal records through your LinkedIn, your resume, and have asked people who know you about your character, etc. You cannot leave behind your ethos, it always comes with you.

Examples:

The Fyre Festival was a music festival that never happened. That event would have taken place in the Bahamas in 2017 and was advertised as luxurious, but in practice, it was nothing more than a farce.

Organized by manager Billy McFarland and co-organized by the rapper Ja Rule, it was promoted by world stars such as Kendall Jenner, Bella Hadid, Alessandra

Ambrósio, and Hailey Baldwin. Among the promised musical attractions were the groups Blink 182 and Major Lazer.

I recommend the Netflix documentary *Fyre Festival*, which shows how Billy used his ethos and his previous company, Magnises, to convince investors, celebrities, and the media that his project was legitimate.

This story also reminds us of the trajectory of Theranos and its founder, Elizabeth Holmes: she was the golden girl from Silicon Valley, considered "the next Steve Jobs," who would revolutionize the healthcare world and who had raised millions of dollars with investors.

Everything in Elizabeth Holmes' story sounded fantastic: she had left halfway through a Chemical Engineering course at Stanford University at age 19 to found Real-Time Cures, which later changed its name to Theranos.

The company claimed to simplify the collection and diagnosis process using only one drop of blood.

With Holmes owning half of the company, she instantly landed on Forbes' list in 2013 at the age of 30 as the youngest multi-millionaire woman... but she did not have the technology. She outsourced everything to other companies that performed the exam in a traditional way. She fooled not only her investors, but the FDA.

Billy McFarland and Elizabeth Holmes are examples of people who raised billions of dollars by selling ethos without having an established product.

However, if Jeff Bezos spoke:

"I am going to create a start-up, and I want US$1,000,"

Without a doubt I would give him US$1,000. Look how many successful things this guy has done. I may not even know what he is going to do, but I trust his ethos; I believe he is going to do something big.

Elizabeth Holmes also did this very well.

"I am a student who left Stanford to create a unique technology in the healthcare market," she said.

She presented panels alongside Bill Clinton, received investments from Tim Draper and Rupert Murdoch (some of the biggest investors in the world), and had nothing!

She fooled the FDA, deceived the press, and deceived everyone. I recommend that you watch *The Inventor: Out for Blood In Silicon Valley*, an HBO documentary about her story.

And how did they do it? They did it using speeches focused on ethos because if I trust your ethos, I do not pay attention to what you are talking about.

Ethos is not necessarily related to academic life or tangible achievements; it is the credibility of what you put on the table. In a political debate, ethos is often put on the schedule. It is always a matter of you questioning the other person's character. It is one of the fallacies that we will see ahead, the *ad hominem*.

We often talk about character, so, one way or another, ethos is very present. It is the first thing we unconsciously think about: why am I going to buy this product this woman is selling? Or what is this guy talking about?

When you bought this book, you saw what I had already done in my life. You saw I had already attracted investments in *Shark Tank*, participated in *The Apprentice*, taught at ESPM University, am a Fellow Researcher at Berkeley Global Society, and work in one of the largest communication groups in the world. This is a metalanguage, a metanarrative. However, you still checked the ethos before deciding whether or not it made sense.

This is my ethos:

If Maytê had this much success in her career, the book's contents must be relevant.

One of the greatest examples of ethos I experienced was when I obtained a visa entitled for Extraordinary Skills (O1) in order to work in the United States. Recommendation letters, awards, published books, mentions in the press: I had to gather more than 350 pages of evidence of what could be a qualified and "extraordinary" career and deliver it to the US immigration department.

Ethos is the first thing we always check in discourse in addition to the one that intuitively comes before logical proof and the pathos itself.

Do I believe in this politician or not?

Do I believe in my leader or not?

Do I believe in this person who is coming to be interviewed for a position in the company?

Do I buy that person's ethos or not?

This has much more to do with reputation and image than with tangible deliverables and data about said individual's achievements.

"Cool, Maytê, but what about the logos?"

It is the logical proof and the reason. It is everything we need to measure, understand, and verify in some way.

LOGOS

So, we are talking about academic sources, scientific research, and data.

Do you know those speeches that start with "90% of women, 50% of men," and "more than three million people"? These speeches try to take people to the field of logic.

So, what is the danger of this speech? If it is 100% logical, it will not captivate your audience.

According to *Neuroscience*, we have the prefrontal and the limbic brain parts. The part that captures data is the neocortex, but what captures our attention, in the region of the limbic system, is emotion, not reason.

LOGOS	ETHOS	PATHOS
Arguments	Personal Antidote	Stories
Benefits	Why me?	Emotions
Facts	Testimony	Emotional Appeal (Anger, Love...)
Images	Witness	Storytelling
Data	Background	Empathy
Statistics	Success Story	Vulnerability
Scientific Research	Credibility	
Processes	Values	
Attributes of Product	Ideology	
Case Study		

So, what I suggest is: you must bring logical proof to your speech. You must prove it. It is what we call "Reason to believe" in advertising.

If I want to make you think that the Amazon is big, I will show you the Amazon map and compare it with the Brazilian territory. If I want to show it in a way that looks small, I am going to show the world map (which is the logical data). It will then look smaller.

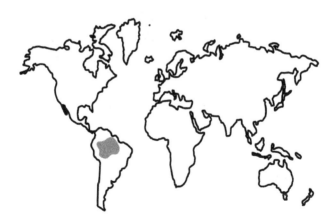

If I want to make a comparison where I make something look small in Brazil, I can compare Brazil with China or India. Both are much more populous countries than Brazil – so anything is going to look smaller, get it?

When you read a news story, when you analyze a chart, when someone shares with you some information, think about these parameters: sometimes they are logical but do not have the slightest logical relationship among themselves. They are presented as logos data, but they are fallacies disguised as reason.

And the heart?

PATHOS

Pathos is about everything that moves us, everything that makes us empathize with the narrative being told.

For each type of subject, there is a different pathos. I would say: when we are giving speeches to a person, sometimes what will work for this person is pathos, which moves the person in the sense of mercy (*ad misericordiam*, which we will see later on). When we are talking to another person, according to the person's profile, mercy will not work. What will work is intimidation or seduction.

All these provocations, seductions, or intimidations depend, however, on our subject. Speeches more oriented by pathos will always provoke an emotion, no matter what.

I will give you an example: a non-governmental organization video. Have you ever seen those ones from Greenpeace and Doctors Without Borders? I can find a video of a turtle in the ocean, squalid, starving, and awaken a bad, alarmist, mercy, scarcity feeling in you. Or I can, for the same cause, show a video of my work, which takes doctors, food, and supplies to that region. I can show these turtles healthier, running, and playing. Then I increment the material, editing it with vivid, saturated colors. Same message, different pathos approach.

Note that I am talking about the same topic. It is a tragic topic, but I can approach it in an alarmist and pessimistic way, or I can sound optimistic and hopeful. There are narratives that can be optimistic or alarming which can scare you or give you a breath of hope.

That is how political speeches, environmental causes, and even start-up pitches tend to be.

You are never going to put your reputation aside; that is why so often, when we see a politician telling a sad story, we are not moved because we are able to judge them and realize through ethos: "I won't buy this pathos." I will not buy this story. Those tears are fake.

Now that you've learned all about ethos, pathos, and logos and how to dose it according to your audience or project, let's learn about the four ways to land them in a speech.

I need you to promise me that next time you have
a job interview
or are at an important meeting
or even a date, whatever it is,
you'll look in the mirror and you'll say
"I hope I like them"
As opposed to
"I hope they like me"

.

3-THE FOUR PERSUASIVE APPROACHES TO PERSUASION

PIST THEORY: Provocation, Intimidation, Seduction, and Temptation

Now that you already know about ethos, pathos, and logos you also need to know of the four styles of narratives and approaches that can be used when wanting to convince someone of something.

Ethos, pathos, and logos are indivisible, and essential to any discourse. However, such speech can be presented in four different ways: provoking, seducing, tempting, or intimidating.

Let us imagine a situation: I want to encourage my son to pass an important test, and I decide to give him a gift if he succeeds. I can get the same message across in completely different ways. Look:

Provocation

A negative image of the competence of the other is created:

I doubt you will pass the test and get a bike.

Intimidation

There is a negative value that represents a threat to the recipient:

If you don't pass the test, you won't get a bike.

Seduction

A positive image of the recipient is created:

You're so smart, I'm sure you'll pass the test and get a bike.

Temptation

The individual offers a positive value:

If you pass the test, you get a bike.

When I want to tempt a person, I offer a positive value to them. So, for example, in the sentence "If you pass the test, you get a bike", I am attaching a positive value to the condition of passing the exam.

For instance, when talking about a painkiller advertisement: "You took this medicine, the pain disappears," I am presenting the positive value: as soon as you take this medicine, your headache goes away.

I could say to you, "If you don't take this medicine, the pain won't go away," but that would be intimidation, which is another style.

So, by analogy, in temptation, I will always offer a positive value to my subject.

"Maytê, how do I know if I'm going to tempt, provoke, intimidate, or seduce?"

The answer is simple: knowing your subject.

It is very important to know your subject. If they are a narcissistic person, seducing them is very effective. If they are an insecure person, there's no way they wanted to be provoked. If they are someone of a more impetuous character, they are worth provoking. Of course, always responsibly! Do not use these tactics in a perverse systematic way.

Each person has a different repertoire and training, and it is necessary to consider the biopsychosocial aspect of the individual:

Social and cultural aspects:

European cultures are different from Latin ones, for example.

Religious:

Judeo-Christian education is different from Eastern education, for example.

Individuals:

An only child? Did they study at a Waldorf school or a military college? Family setting and principles taught in early, second, and third childhood are important.

We reproduce the dynamics we readily know. It is very common if you have a mother or father who approaches you in a passive-aggressive way, to reproduce this with your friends and in your relationships.

Observe your speech pattern and approach, and know your subject's pattern too. What can be considered good for your upbringing, education, and culture can be offensive to someone else's. So, it is important to know our subject so as to not generate cognitive dissonance in our message. This is a basic principle of Communication Theory.

Since moving to the United States, I have also changed the way I approach people, especially at work.

An author I really like, called Max Weber, wrote a book titled *The Protestant Ethic and the Spirit of Capitalism*. In this book, he addresses how American culture is more self/individual-focused, meritocratic in a philosophical and empirical sense, and pragmatic. According to him, for Protestants, work is a means to prosper, while for the Catholics it is a punishment for having eaten the forbidden fruit.

Brazil, in turn, colonized by Portugal with an evangelization carried out by the Roman Catholic Church, carries with it a pang of certain guilt linked to prosperity and work: as if usury and profit were a sin.

Why am I saying all this?

CONTEXT

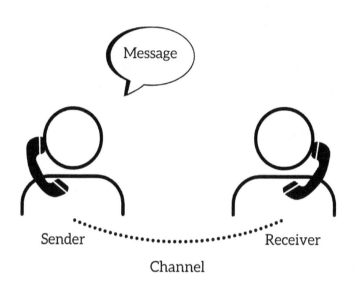

Because it changes everything. Here, in the United States, my communication is direct, and straightforward, without too many layers of narration. What is considered assertive here, many Latinxs would consider rude or too straightforward. These small subtleties and touches facilitate my communication because I am using words from their repertoire to communicate and generate a clear and noise-free message.

Now let's address Intimidation:

If I were to use intimidation in the same sentence as "If you pass the entrance exam...," I would say "If you don't pass the entrance exam, you don't get the bike."

This change is very simple, but I would be threatening the receptor. It is tied to a negative value for the receptor. Intimidation works when offering a negative character to my subject.

The example of intimidation is not always linked to a threat. By saying "If you don't pass, you don't get a bike," intimidation is much subtler and more subliminal. We are often intimidated and do not even notice. We are intimidated by girlfriends, boyfriends, partners, bosses, mothers, fathers, and more.

Intimidation can be more subliminal or more straightforward. When we talk about fallacies, you will notice this. The *ad baculum* fallacy, whose name comes from the war hammer, is a fallacy that works a lot in the field of intimidation.

Provocation, on the other hand, will literally lead the subject to doubts.

So, following our example: "I doubt you'll pass the entrance exam to get a bike." Look how strong this is! I am provoking, questioning the competence of the other. It is also a negative image of the competence of the other person and not of what I am going to link to this person.

I am not saying "you're not going to get a bike;" the point is that I, the sender of the message, doubt the other's competence to do so.

Last but not least, seduction. I would say that in the majority of marketing cases of politicians, advertising, and also in our daily personal exchanges, seduction is the most used type of narrative.

Nowadays we live in a world where the spirit of time is narcissistic. It is almost a pathology, I would add.

A wonderful book that I love and recommend addresses this: *Plaire et toucher: Essai sur la société de séduction*, by the French philosopher Gilles Lipovetsky.

Lipovetsky's book addresses the practice of seduction in all spheres of current society, showing that pleasing and impressing are mandatory verbs. The work reflects on the art of seduction in times of hypermodernity, not only in the sexual and relationships sphere but also in the way we consume, in politics, education, and social networks, among others.

According to the author, please and impress have become mandatory verbs, abandoning other forms of interrelation.

Here is then an invitation for a mature reflection on the society in which we live: if narcissism seems to be epidemic in times of Instagram and the likes of it, and a persuasive approach to seduction is increasingly present, how can we shield ourselves and know ourselves in order to avoid falling into this narrative either as a subject or a receiver of the message?

Another recent example is the Korean film *Parasite*, in which we notice the seductive narrative in many of the script's dialogues. This is the main narrative used in the dialogues between the Kim and Park families. In my opinion, they go beyond the considered healthy limits of persuasive technique and border on psychopathy.

Let us analyze three elements present in the dialogs (spoiler alert!):

1. Triangulation

When Ki-Taek, the patriarch of the family who serves the Park family, hands over a card from a supposed home care company, he is indirectly triangulating his wife's recommendation. In addition, he values himself to Mr. Park when he says: "They approached me to work for someone else." This is a classic example of triangulation, in which, by appearing to be an object of desire for the subject, subject B becomes interesting for subject A.

It is that Freudian notion of desire: we no longer want what we want, but instead, want what we lack, what others have. It's the pursuit of desire. This is why nightclubs with big lines are more desired, and so is the last piece of the cake. If everyone wants it, it must be the best and I, too, must have it.

2. Scarcity and urgency

When Kevin endorses Jessica to the madam as an art teacher, he says: "I have to check if she has room in her schedule because she's been too busy." This triggers a sense of scarcity and urgency. The "Only tomorrow!" makes us feel pressured to take action. Since the issue at hand proves to be scarce, it generates an urgency for decision-making. This tactic is also widely used in advertising.

3. Isopraxism

In several scenes of the film, we note that the characters of the Kim family imitate the most used words (in a specific scene they even decorate lines) by the Parks in order to generate rapport. Isopraxism is the act of copying or mirroring the other to comfort them which generates trust through the mimesis of vocabulary or even bodily gestures.

The narcissist likes to be seduced. So instead of saying "If you don't pass, I won't give you a car" or "I doubt you'll pass to get a car", you say: "You are so clever! I'm sure you'll pass the entrance exam and get a car."

The sender is creating a positive image of the person: "I seduce in the sense of praising, in the sense of embracing, acting on the person's vulnerability and not playing vulnerability against itself," which is what the bully does, what the person who has doubts does.

I recognize your virtues and, because of that, I know that everything will be all right.

This is a case where, many times, it is not even necessary to be explicit. Often when I talk about seduction, people think it is a course by Hitch, The Love Counselor. Those practices of how to meet and conquer any woman, any man... "Speak with a voice like that..." That is not it!

The seducer, by definition, is a person who will make a positive image of the other person and who will listen much more to the subject.

They are going to empathize, or, sometimes, they are going to emulate empathy. Because there are a lot of psychopaths who emulate empathy, it is very difficult to identify them. (Careful! You must be attentive and observe!)

He will listen to your story, he will show he cares, he will pay attention to you (which is our most valuable asset today: our attention, our time), and with the information you give him, then yes, he will seduce you.

In the United States, my communication is direct,
without too many layers of narration.
What is considered assertive here,
many Latinxs would consider rude
or too straightforward.
It's all about cultural nuances and respecting them.

PERSUASION

4- THIS IS A FALLACY!

HOW TO SPOT THEM AND AVOID FALLING INTO ONE

Now that you have read about ethos, pathos, logos, and the four styles of approach, it is time for us to get to know one more layer in the wonderful world of persuasion: fallacy. Fallacy is an even more tactile layer of speech.

It is important to know fallacies because they are used all the time. We live in an era where a lot of fake news is consumed. They tell us lies by telling us only half-truths.

How many times have we not been led, especially by the media or politicians, to have an opinion that we believed to be impartial but was loaded with bias and hidden intentions? To compare countries using per capita criteria, for example, one needs to consider the population. If a country is much more populous, everything will always look bigger.

Each image and word choice is a code, but additionally, comparisons, examples, and even correlations made in a narrative do not always imply causality.

Next time someone says something to you, from politicians to newspaper news, be suspicious. Compared to what? What is the parameter? Is there any research that crosses the two indicators mentioned separately? What method is used?

In the era of click bait, subterfuges can come with the face of news, and the most difficult fake news to perceive is the one based on real information, even if it is illogical and fallacious.

"Is this bad or good, Maytê?"

I do not want to judge here. The thing is that, even if subconsciously, we also use fallacies.

I want to get you all on the same page; therefore, I am going to start with one of the fallacies that I consider the most latent and present today: the *ad hominem* fallacy.

FALLACIES

1. Ad hominem: abusive, circumstantial, and *tu quoque*

The *ad hominem* fallacy directly attacks the character of the person who is the subject of the message. In this fallacy, I do not question the agenda that is being addressed but instead, the ethos, the credibility, the character of who is speaking, and what is being talked about.

There are three types of the *ad hominem* fallacy:

ABUSIVE

CIRCUMSTANTIAL

TU QUOQUE

To explore these types, we will use the following style of conversation as an example:

ABUSIVE AD HOMINEM

Ad personam consists of a direct personal attack on the character of the person who proposed a given argument.

In this dialogue, no one is talking about sugar generating an endorphin and dopamine release action in the brain, and therefore being addictive. We are not talking about sugar or the sugar process. I just say: "You drink!"

It is like someone saying: "Avoid eating fat because it's bad for your health." And another person replies: "You smoke! What do you know about health?"

Abusive *ad hominem* directly questions a person's character.

On the other hand, the circumstantial *ad hominem* will question the context.

Person A will say:

"Eating sugar is bad for your health."

Person B will reply:

"You say that because your family owns an aspartame factory. You sell sweeteners, and that's why you're saying sugar is bad for health. You have an economic, political interest."

CIRCUMSTANTIAL AD HOMINEM

Ad hominem circumstantiae is when the partiality of the person who proposed the argument is called into question, indicating that the person would have something to gain by defending a certain point of view.

Questioning is the circumstantial *ad hominem*, which is also an attack on the person's morals, but it is not abusive: it is circumstantial. It is important to remember the context, okay?

The third and most classic is the *tu quoque*. It's the famous: "Hey, you too!"

TU QUOQUE AD HOMINEM

It is also known as the fallacy of hypocrisy because the opponent is accused of doing what the opponent is calling into question.

It is known as a fallacy of hypocrisy, when your opponent in the debate says, "You do that too!"

Following the same example:

Person A says:

"Eating sugar is bad for your health."

Person B replies:

"Hey, but you also eat sugar every day! You eat cake. Do you think that the cake you eat does not have sugar?"

It is the famous "you too."

An example of this in pop culture is in the movie, *The Devil Wears Prada*. Whoever has watched it can remember Miranda Priestly when she ends up sacrificing her friend's promotion to keep her job.

Andrea, played by Anne Hathaway, gets in the car and chides the boss: "Miranda, how dare you do this? He was your friend!" Miranda replies: "Honey, how did I have the courage to do this? You just did this to Emily".

The issue in question is not brought up; instead, the character of the speaker is questioned: politicians use this type of fallacy in debates a lot, for example.

In short, the different categories of ad hominem fallacies are:

Abusive ad hominem (ad personam)

It is a direct personal attack on the character of the argument's proponent.

Circumstantial ad hominem (ad hominem circustantiae)

The ability of the argument's proponent is called into question, indicating that the proponent would have something to gain by defending a given point of view.

Tu quoque

The fallacy of hypocrisy, as the adversary is accused of having the same habit.

2. Ad Baculum

Another fallacy that is widely used these days, especially in politics, is the *ad baculum* fallacy: the argument of the hammer, a coercive argument.

It is as if we were, in a way, intimidating the others and appealing to consequences through fear.

By creating fear, by citing strength, I manipulate you to do what I want, to give me what I want also using my ethos, my authority.

Generally, people who use *ad baculum* have a very strong ethos.

It is very difficult to find an intimidating person with a weak ethos. Without it, the person would be unable to generate fear in you. So, what causes fear in the *ad baculum* fallacy is the power the subject has.

It is what makes us think: man, if I don't do what they want, if everything they say doesn't happen, I'm screwed. It is noteworthy that this person is usually very powerful.

Ad baculum is a fallacy of intimidation, a fallacy of strength.

AD BACULUM

The appeal to strength (lit. *argumentum ad baculum*): argument of the hammer is a fallacy in which force and coercion are presented as arguments to agree with the author of the conclusion. It can also be related to the appeal to authority using the power of being an authority in a given situation to convince someone of an argument.

John Doe, a famous politician, **tweets**:

If you vote for Jane Doe, our country will be doomed to unemployment and failure. People will starve to death. Do you really want to vote for Jane and let the country collapse?

3. Ad Populum

The *ad populum* – which comes from the Latin "appeal to the crowd" – works the fallacious model according to quantity.

Unlike that fallacy in which we put fear, in *ad populum* I say:

"Nine out of ten dentists approve of the X toothpaste brand". Note that I am not saying, for example, that a famous and renowned doctor recommends it, (which is another fallacy we will cover next). I am saying: "Several doctors recommend it." I appeal to quantity to justify whether something is good or bad.

AD POPULUM

Argumentum ad populum is a Latin expression that defines a fallacious reasoning that consists in saying that a certain proposition is valid or good simply because many people, or the vast majority, approve of it. It is also called appeal to quantity; the argument is invalid because nothing guarantees that something is true or correct just because of its popularity.

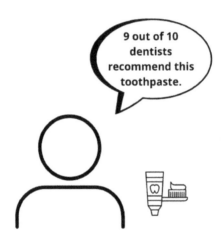

4. Ad Verecundiam

Opposite to *ad populum* is *ad verecundiam*, which is a discourse 100% based on the ethos of what I am referring to.

In it, I say: "This famous and renowned doctor uses this toothpaste", for example.

It would be like the pope saying that the Church agrees that divorce is acceptable. I am not saying that most priests said they agree with divorce in the Catholic Church: I am using the pope, the ultimate authority in that system.

The *ad verecundiam* fallacy will always work a false logic linked to authority.

When I throw a very valuable ethos in my subject's face, it tends not to reflect critically. The subject does not reflect intelligently on the editorial content that is presented. I buy the idea for its ethos, for its *ad verecundiam*. It is a fallacy that evokes a lot of ethos.

So, when I see a celebrity saying, "I bought this brand of car", or "I bought this lipstick", there is an appeal to authority. Advertising uses this appeal a lot.

AD VERECUNDIAM

The *argumentum ad verecundiam*, or *argumentum magister dixit*, is a Latin expression meaning appeal to authority or an authority argument.

It is a logical fallacy that appeals to the speech or the reputation of some authority in order to validate the argument.

Joana tweets:

Even Dr. John Doe agrees that this is unacceptable! If he says so, it must be true.

5. Ad misericordiam

A fallacy often used mainly by children is the *ad misericordiam*, which is the appeal to mercy, literally speaking.

It is almost like blackmail, for example: "I would be so happy if I got a puppy! I'm not happy only because I don't have a puppy, if you don't get me a puppy I will fail at school".

Also, many adults use *ad misericordiam*: in a subtle way and a little more subliminally, but they do. It is a fallacy that evokes the "pity" of the subject and victimizes the sender of the message.

The fact is that *ad misericordiam* evokes a more pathos side. It is, therefore, a narrative that evokes feelings.

AD MISERICORDIAM

Appealing to mercy (Latin: *argumentum ad misericordiam*) is a fallacy. It consists in gaining the opponent's sympathy by presenting yourself as a person worthy of pity.

6. False dilemma

It is a fallacy often used in personal relationships involving an abusive bias. The false dilemma presents us with a dichotomy that does not really exist.

A common phrase: "Whoever is not with me is against me." Or even a political slogan seen during Brazil's dictatorship: "Brazil: love it or leave it."

I may not love Brazil because I know all of its economic, environmental, and social problems, but I do not necessarily have to leave it. I can continue there fighting, exercising my active voice, demanding accountability from politicians.

Why do I have to love or leave my country? To be more easily guided as a citizen?

The narrative often has a bias of control, of persuasion - even in the political sphere. We need to be aware of false dichotomies, false dilemmas.

"Whoever is not with me is against me." "It's either me or your job." "It's either me or your friends and your weekend getaway."

Folks, I will give you an important tip: run away from this. If someone keeps using that kind of approach with you, run away!

7. Hasty generalization

The fallacy of hasty generalization tends to be somewhat reductionist.

Hasty generalization is nothing more than taking exceptions as rules or taking stereotypes – often with prejudice – as well as society's traces and turning them into maxims. So, when I say: "This is a woman thing," "This is a man thing," "Women do this, men do that," "Men wear blue, women wear pink," I am making a hasty generalization.

Let me give you an example: in the previous topic, I talked about false dilemmas. Sometimes a person grew up listening to his father and mother saying something. Or the person had a teacher in early, second, or third childhood who often said something.

HASTY GENERALIZATION

It is also known as the fallacy of unqualified generalization and fallacy of accident.

Simplistic rules or laws rarely take legitimate exceptions into account, and to ignore these exceptions is to ignore reality in order to preserve the illusion of a perfect law. People like simplicity and often prefer to keep simplicity at the expense of rationality.

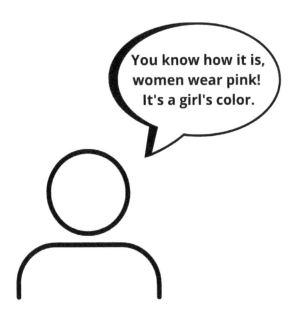

8. Post hoc

It is a very curious fallacy widely used by the media, politicians, and in relationships in general.

POST HOC ERGO PROPTER HOC

Just because event A happens at the same time as event B, it does not mean that A caused B. Determining whether there is, in fact, a causality relationship requires further investigation, as five situations may occur in this case:

1. A really causes B;

2. B could be the cause of A;

3. A third fact C may be causing both A and B;

4. It may be a combination of the first two situations above.
   For example:
   A causes B and, at the same time, B causes A;

5. The correlation may just be a coincidence, meaning that the two events have no relationship other than the fact that they occur at the same time.

   In scientific studies, using a large sample helps to reduce the likelihood of a coincidence.

Ear Cancer Growth

Incidence of ear cancer   Increased use of smartphones

1. Over the past 10 years, the cases of ear cancer have increased.
2. Over the past 10 years, smartphones have been popularized.

Therefore, smartphones cause ear cancer.

9. Reversal of burden of proof

An argument based on reversing the burden of proof generally takes the following form:

I state something.

You do not accept this statement.

So, you must prove it to be false.

Therefore, the logical order is inverted, which should be:

I state something. You do not accept it. So, I must prove it to be true.

That is, arguer A makes a statement but is not willing to prove it, transferring to opponent B the obligation to do so.

There is also a subtler form of reversal when two people each make a claim and one of them demands the other to prove that the denial of his claim is correct. For example:

A: Science is the only source of truth.

B: Religion is the only source of truth.

A: Prove me that science is not the only source of truth.

B: Prove me that religion is not the only source of truth.

In the example above, both arguers applied the reversal of the burden of proof against each other.

Legally, the reversal of the burden of proof is applied when the accuser is the weakest party. Example: a former employee claims that she worked after her shift; the former employer must present the timecards to prove that this is not true.

10. False analogy

False analogy is when the similarity between two objects is the starting point for a conclusion. Surely you have already fallen for it and/or used it.

I joke that it is like the comparison of oranges to apples: both have the common trait of being fruits, but both are different.

How difficult is it for us to realize that we are falling into a false analogy? It is because it looks legitimate. It sounds logical, but it is not.

It is practically a sophistry.

Sophistry is the argument or reasoning conceived with the aim of producing the illusion of truth, which, although it simulates agreement with the rules of logic, actually presents an inconsistent, incorrect, and deliberately misleading internal structure.

Example: why can't students consult materials while taking an exam? Every student should take an exam and bring books to consult them. Because, after all, when the doctor is going to give a clinical diagnostic opinion, she has the documents and the exams at hand to be consulted. A lawyer can carry a penal code book to an appointment with the client or even in court.

Why can the student not bring a book during the exam?

Does that kind of statement not seem a bit legitimate?

What is the incongruity?

The lawyer and the doctor have already graduated; therefore, they are not in a period of training and passing tests. Therefore, they have already proven that they are able to exercise that career.

Thus, consultation is not required for him to pass a test. Not the student: the student needs to pass the test in order to be able to practice the career.

It is very easy to fall into a false analogy. Hence, we always have to understand whether the arguments have similarities that are actually congruent or are just random assumptions used to deceive the argument or discourse.

In the era of click bait, subterfuges can come with the face of news, and the most difficult fake news to perceive is the one based on real information, even if it is illogical and fallacious.

.

5-PERSUASIVE SPEECH IN BUSINESS: PITCH

Before getting into the tactical and strategic part of how to structure a persuasive narrative of a pitch, it is necessary that I go over information about mindset, mentality, and beliefs. That is because a lot of what makes us persuasive is our state of mind.

If you do a pitch or a presentation or sell some project or idea and you are shy, introverted, feeling bad - if you do not feel confident in what you are going to say, and I am not just talking about body posture, but if in your head you feel like an impostor, inferior - then forget it. There is no persuasion book in the world that will help you!

Therefore, it is necessary to work on some issues.

I offer here some tactics that have helped me a lot every time I have done an important presentation or faced a meeting with someone who is super-powerful, very rich, or very famous. Michelle Obama once said, "I've been sitting at tables with the most powerful people in the world, and believe me, they're not that smart".

I believe that.

Sometimes, we idealize and get scared and reticent, but it does not have to be like that!

People are people. We need to understand this. They have their weaknesses, their demons, their vices, and their virtues.

The second tip I would give is: money is a commodity. It does not matter if the guy is a billionaire. If he is in front of you, if he took fifteen minutes out of his day to give you, in those minutes, in that time, your hour is worth the same price.

No one's time is worth more than another's!

If they have taken the time to talk to you, use it to your advantage. And think that no matter how wealthy the other person is, he or she only has money.

It is just money.

What you know, who you know, what you have studied, the times you have been dumped or laid off, the traumas you have been through... that is yours only. Only you experienced them.

The privilege of a lifetime is being who you are.

Money does not buy it, it is intangible.

We have to value the intangible.

Some people are in the habit of letting others wait for hours on end before receiving them.

If someone does this to you, setting up a meeting at 4:00 pm but receiving you at 4:30 pm with the largest poker face saying: "Look, sorry, I was late," you should reply: "Don't worry, I set aside an hour of my day for this meeting. So, we're going to have this meeting in half an hour, okay?"

Oops. I regained power.

Control your time, value the time of others, respect the time of others.

Another mindset tip: several million-dollar ideas were turned down.

I will tell you a secret: yours will be too! Does that mean it is bad? No! It means that your idea is not in line with that fund investment's thesis, that the investor profile is different from your business proposal. It may mean so much beyond simply saying that such an idea is a bad one.

For example, Rocío van Nierop, the cofounder and executive director of the advocacy group Latinas in Tech, visited the tech accelerator Y Combinator. She noticed that the teams that Y Combinator had funded were all white men. This experience led her to publish a database of Latina entrepreneurs who had raised at least $1 million to show aspiring founders that they existed. She got funded, nevertheless, she persisted.

You cannot give up or think your project is bad just because of constructive criticism. You need to learn from it, see if it makes sense, and put the feedback into practice (or not). You do not need to take advantage of all feedback you get, ok?

Not all criticism is constructive. You need to know how to filter it. "How am I supposed to know that, Maytê?"

First: know yourself.

Second: know your strengths and weaknesses.

Third: know your project.

If you know what you are selling, your idea, your project, a project within your company, whatever it is, if you know it and you own it, you know the sense that it makes.

Go ahead. Do not listen to haters. Haters and critics are not in the arena. There is a saying I love from the speech, "The Man in the Arena" (or "Citizenship in a Republic") delivered by Theodore Roosevelt at the Sorbonne on April 23, 1910.

> "It is not the critic who counts; not the man who points out how the strong man stumbles, or where the doer of deeds could have done them better...The credit belongs to the man who is actually in the arena, whose face is marred by dust and sweat and blood; who strives valiantly; who errs, who comes short again and again, because there is no effort without error and shortcoming; but who does actually strive to do the deeds; who knows great enthusiasms, the great devotions; who spends himself in a worthy cause; who at the best knows in the end the triumph of high achievement, and who at the worst, if he fails, at least fails while daring greatly".

Last but not least: stop playing small. It does not help the world at all.

"Oh, thank you so much for having me, and thank you so much for giving me a little bit of your time. I know you are a very busy person!"

No! Go head-to-head.

Smile, be nice without being arrogant, but stop playing small. As an immigrant and a Latina, so many times I felt embarrassed of my broken English or strong accent. I decided to own it. This is what makes me who I am.

Stop self-deprecating!

Did you receive a compliment? Did you get a feedback? Thank the person. Own it.

When you shine, you immediately authorize others around you to shine too. Instead of staying in that cloud of mediocrity, let us all be brilliant, powerful. That way, you allow others to shine too.

Do not shrink yourself to fit in a place
that is not your size.
And, especially,
if you see that you are bigger than that space,
go away.

You should not think, "I hope investors like me", but rather, "I hope I like these investors. I hope I like this person who is going to interview me for this job vacancy. I hope their values, beliefs, and worldviews are aligned with mine – and if not, I won't stay there".

I want you to promise me that the next time you have a job interview or an important meeting to present a project, or even a date with that app crush you still do not know, whatever it is, you will look in the mirror and say: "I hope I like them", and not: "I hope they like me".

For a long time in our lives, on the first day of school, or moving to a new country, new culture, where we are tested, we wanted to be accepted, to belong, to win applause. When we put ourselves in a place of choosing, we regain the active voice and the leading role in our lives. It is not about acting superior or being arrogant but acting on an equal footing with our subject.

How to make a pitch

Now that you are an expert in rhetorical resources and narrative fallacies, I would like to move on to a very important module for you who work doing presentations, be they investment pitches for your company, a new project you would like to put out in your area, or even a side project you want to carry out.

I am going to bring you some news that is good, but worrisome. I do not know if anyone has ever told you, but no one is interested in your idea. Not as much as you are.

It is hard to read that, isn't it?

We spend so much time thinking, dreaming, reading, studying, doing. And, when we are going to make our pitch, we think that everyone is interested in the subject that we study and like so much.

They are not.

So, this is a basic premise when we are going to do a presentation, yet here I am talking about structure, the storytelling, and the slides you are going to show. No one is interested in your idea as much as you are.

Therefore, starting from this premise, it is possible to capture the attention of our subject, our audience.

The first tip I will give is: start the presentation provocatively – and I would avoid asking questions, okay?

Why? What happens when you ask questions? You may be shooting yourself in the foot. "Who has never had a problem opening a legal entity account?" Man, if you do not know your audience and if they had a problem with it or not, there is going to be that lonely hay ball rolling among the audience and you are going to be super embarrassed and lose your audience at that point.

So, I personally think it is a rip-off for you to start with questions.

Even cliché questions such as, "Who here wants to be rich and healthy?" Everyone will raise their hand, got it? So, it becomes something embarrassing. Rather than start by asking these kinds of questions, which may lose the audience's attention, I would tell you to start in a provocative way.

Why?

Because provocation makes the person stop thinking about the bills or counting the tiles on the wall and pay attention to what you are talking about.

When you put on a more provocative slide, you can truly capture your listener's attention.

So, I always like to make something more cryptic.

When I made the pitch for b.pass (a beauty classpass), my startup, I wrote: "Beauty matters". And I did not say anything else. There was only the slide there.

Then, one looked at each other's faces, and I saw it was generating tension.

Anything that generates tension, generates attention.

So, I started by saying: "Beauty matters. It matters so much that in Brazil the beauty market is greater than health care and basic education in addressable market sizes. We are the third largest consumer of beauty in the world..."

I began provocatively, subversively.

The third aspect of any storytelling narrative's pitch, especially if it is more persuasive, is to dramatize the problem.

This will make you generate empathy in your subject.

THE PROBLEM

Dramatize the problem with big numbers and complete with a vision of the industry, the market, and the future.

Getting the listener into the problem, even if she does not fit the right persona, in other words, the kind of people who suffer from this type of challenge, is key.

When I dramatize, I manage to generate even more empathy in the sense of tangibility, when I say: "Wow, I did not know women had so much difficulty and spent so much on beauty brands. I did not know, I have never bought nail polish, I have never painted my nails..."

Now you can imagine what it was like for me to be able to make an investment pitch for my start-up in a meeting dominated by men. I had to get them to walk in my shoes, so to speak.

As you can see, I always like to show everything big: big numbers, big pictograms that summarize your problem, etc.

Dramatize the problem. Write a sentence about changing the market with a visual appeal.

"X million people, X million dollars, ten billion stores," the main problems that still exist and that your company or project intends to solve.

A brief explanation of the problem, in a way.

So, applying my former app b.pass example:

"The beauty market makes 100 billion... There are so many women who find it difficult to schedule a visit... A thousand procedures that are carried out a year in Brazil. And the market is asymmetrical, fragmented, and consolidating" etc. Thus, I can show highlights and lead my subject's cognitive process towards understanding what I am saying through these visual resources.

The fourth is the market size.

What is market size? It is the rationale for you to be able to show, especially if you are an investor, that the market is large enough to justify an investment.

So, this is the market share I am going to reach. Here you can measure whether we are talking about a billion-dollar or a million-dollar or a multi-million-dollar market. I use orders of magnitude for this market.

MARKET SIZE	
TAM	TOTAL ADDRESSABLE MARKET
SAM	SPECIFIC ADDRESSABLE MARKET
SOM	SPECIFIC OBTAINABLE MARKET

MILLIONS   BILLIONS   **BILLIONS**

Because, often, the investor will ask: "How big is this thing?" If I do not understand this market, I cannot quantify it.

And there you are, already showing the person who is willing to invest whether or not you fit their investment thesis.

The fifth aspect is the solution. And it happens, mainly, with projects that are incipient.

You have identified a problem you want to solve with your start-up, with your project, with your movie, but you have not created the right project yet. You are still at a very early stage.

Then you sell, sell the project, sell the problem, but when it is time to sell the solution, you speak quickly, looking down, and show no more than one slide.

Guys, stop everything. You have to give the same importance to the solution as you give to the problem.

No use saying: "Maria wanted to rent a car, tried the market leader, and couldn't rent it because it was too expensive; she tried elsewhere, and couldn't do it, so I created the solution for a fast and cheap car." Next slide. No!

If you have dramatized the problem, dramatize the solution as well.

And then everything is fine. You have to give it the same weight, otherwise it becomes asymmetrical.

SOLUTION

Focus. Show investors that you are down to earth.

The problem can be multiple; the solution is only one.

Avoid clichés.

It is no use showing a big, hideously enormous problem and coming up with a small solution. It is necessary that the solution lives up to the problem.

It is also very important, when you are going to show a solution, to not just stay in an intangible field of value proposition, mission, vision, and values.

So, if you show your job to be done, think: to what problem will your solution be hired to solve?

I like to give an example to talk about job to be done, which is: if I want to hang a picture on the wall, I can hang it with a drill, duct tape, or with a nail and a hammer.

Each has a different value proposition. One does not get things around dirty; the other is easier; the other is even more work. Although proposed with different values, their job to be done is the same. It is a picture on the wall. My job to be done is to hang the painting on the wall, and all three solutions aim to do that.

Therefore, I encourage you to think about the job to be done not only considering its value proposition; thus, you will be able to realize the solution that your project or your company offers much better.

Product. Here, my friends, it is time to shine, to imagine yourself at the presentation listening to that "ohhhhhh"... get it?

Show a wonderful slide of your product, of your service, use it and abuse it; if it is a software, if it is an app, try to show it in use.

PRODUCT DEMO

Anything you can do that enhances your platform, your solution, this is the time to use it.

If you already have traction... What is traction? It is: "I had 50 users, now I have 100, 150." It is where you show how much you have grown and how much you are earning.

And it is where you show the customer base, the recurring value – each business and each project have a different performance indicator; these are KPIs (Key Performance Indicators).

Choose yours and show them.

Graphics here are very welcome. Especially if it is a graph that ascends, of growth (because if is a descending graph, I suggest you improve your business and actually grow your base).

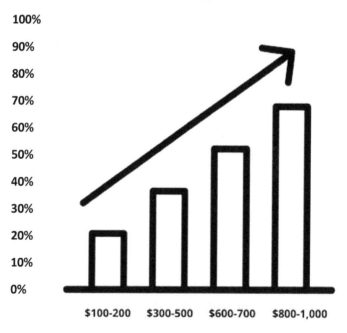

TRACTION

Customer Base / Recurring Value

GRAPH THAT SHOWS GROWTH

Business model. What is it like to monetize it?

I have seen several presentations that talk, talk, talk, but do not tell you how you are going to make money. Is it the marketplace? Is it e-commerce? Is it a software? Do you earn for the transaction? Do you get paid for a subscription? How do you monetize? Where does money come in and where does money go out?

BUSINESS MODEL

Business Model / Customer Lifecycle			
CLIENT A	XYZ	XYZ	XYZ
CLIENT B	XYZ	XYZ	XYZ
CLIENT C	XYZ	XYZ	XYZ

HOW TO MONETIZE

When it comes to NGOs, it is not a project that seeks to monetize the action. It is a solidary project belonging to the third sector. This has to be in your performance indicator in a way that can be made tangible.

If it is a software, how many people have unsubscribed? These data points are important. The number of new users per month is important.

If it is a marketplace, what is the acquisition cost per user? In other words: how much does it cost for you to bring a user to your base? How long does the user spend at your base? It is the most important data point in this case.

Your differential is our sixth point.

What do you have that your competitor does not have?

What makes you different or better than others?

I think it is always very productive to put a chart of your company, your project, and of those that already exist on the market. This is called benchmarking, where you are going to get a little bit more into the details, but, of course, without going overboard.

COMPETITIVE ADVANTAGES

	USABILITY	ATTRIBUTES	PORTFOLIO	CAPILLARITY
YOUR START-UP	XYZ	XYZ	XYZ	XYZ
START-UP A	XYZ	XYZ	XYZ	XYZ
START-UP B	XYZ	XYZ	XYZ	XYZ
START-UP C	XYZ	XYZ	XYZ	XYZ

WHAT MAKES YOU DIFFERENT FROM OTHERS

Vision. This is very important.

You need to show that what you have been doing for six months or a year is based on a long-term view.

Show you are in it to win.

It is necessary to present how this market will gain in the future. Will it consolidate? Will the spec base go down? Will it go international? On what premises are you creating this?

You also need to understand logical-strategic reasoning, the famous assumptions. What are the assumptions you are taking into account to do this?

So, selling a vision is showing that you have a future. Showing that you literally have a long-term view.

How do you see this project six months from now? One year from now?

NEXT STEPS

	2 MONTHS	6 MONTHS	12 MONTHS	24 MONTHS
PRODUCT	XYZ	XYZ	XYZ	XYZ
BUSINESS MODEL	$1M	$2M	$3M	$5M
MARKETING	$500K	$800K	$1M	$2.5M

SHORT AND MEDIUM TERM FORECASTS

If you are raising money, the famous fundraising (attracting investment funds), you will not write that you are asking for money, ok?

You are offering an opportunity! Reframe how to say it. Explain how you will use this money, what the goals are etc.

"I need 500 thousand dollars to expand my marketing and sales team".

"Today I am only earning so much because I can no longer have the capital to invest in the funding base. If I have X, I get Y; if I have 2X, I get 2Y. That is what I need to invest this money for".

Forecast of numbers: the golden rule is that you make logical and concrete projections.

NUMBERS

	2019	2020	2021	2022
USERS	10K	500K	1M	2M
REVENUE	$1M	$2M	$3M	$5M
NET INCOME	$600K	$800K	$1M	$2.5M

CONCRETE NUMBERS BASED ON THE HISTORY AND THE ASSUMPTIONS OF THE BUSINESS PLAN

Five hundred million dollars? Based on what?

Who will win this fight is another aspect of it?

As we said, ethos is very important. What is the ethos of the people who are with you on this journey?

The investor, when putting money in, especially if it is a start-up, which is a very incipient project, surely knows that the project will change along the way.

Now, another uncertainty they have, which is the only thing they will not change – at least, the chances of changing are smaller – is the people who are running the project, the partners.

So, it is time for you to show your resume, the companies you have worked for, the cool projects you have done, who the directors are, and what is going to become of this company.

It is time for you to sell your ethos.

TEAM   **DIRECTORS**

Founder X   Founder Y   Name

bio highlights   bio highlights

You have to be strategic in this decision. You should not say: "When I was 12, I won the Math Olympiad", because unless you are a mathematician and your project is about math, that does not add up too much of the story.

You went there, started high, dramatized, presented the solution, said who are the people who are going to get into this fight, who is going to do it, who is going to happen, and you are going to end with "That's it!"? No! Finish high and say what you really want.

"And that's why I'm here looking for investment, mentorship, partnerships, and advice." Say what you want and end with a call to action, which is an invitation to action.

In my pitch, I said: "And I want to know who of you is going to get into this smart choice with us."

I did not say "this is it." I made a call to action. It started high, it ends high.

Pitch types:

Vision, Team, Tech, and Traction

If we were to divide the types of pitches, mainly talking about start-ups or companies, I would say that there are four different types.

Vision Pitch:

Generally, this type of pitch works when you and your co-founder have a very good view of the market (it is in consolidation, or fragmented, or analog, or in full digitization...). You have a very clear reading of the market from those who have experience in the segment: these are pitches usually made by professionals who have worked for ten, 15 years in a specific sector and are able to do enough reading on market patterns and research to predict some movements in the segment, hence, vision.

Early-stage start-ups in accelerators and with angel investments usually use this type of discourse.

Tech Pitch:

This is the classic "Silicon Valley" pitch, where the technology itself can be more valuable as an asset than the team/vision: most companies are focused on deep tech, something like "supertechs".

Team Pitch:

This pitch is when you have sold ten companies, are a multimillionaire, are going to launch a new company, all while you still do not really know what it is going to be like, but you are still opening a round of fundraising for those who want to be team players.

When you are buying the founder, it means it is a very ethos-focused pitch.

An example of a team pitch was when the founders of 99 Taxis decided to create Yellow, a shared bicycle service. Investors must have thought: if they manage to sell 99 Taxis for $1 billion, I will want to be with them in their next venture. And the Monashees fund invested right at the beginning of Yellow's project (there were 99 investors, too).

Traction Pitch

It is when my partner and I are average people, we do not have a vision outside the box, no big technology, but we are already earning and growing more than 30% per month. You then sell the traction of the idea.

Ideally, you can have a company that is so solid, so good, that it fits all four types. You have a brilliant vision of the market, your team is incredible, and, on top of that, you manage to have traction (because you sell and hit targets), and you have very good technology.

There, my friend, you are invincible.

Now is the time to remember that there is no pitch, or miracle, which makes a bad company look good without solidity or real facts to be evidenced. Work hard, invest your time and energy and own the room as a result!

As an immigrant and a Latina,
so many times I felt embarrassed of my broken English
or strong accent.
I decided to own it.
This is what makes me who I am.

.

6- BODY LANGUAGE:

BE PRESENT

According to neuroscience, opinions are formed about you within the first five seconds of meeting, and many times you have not yet opened your mouth. Sometimes it can be your posture: a hand in your pocket, a gasping breath, a shaking leg, anxiety, or fear that I sense.

Therefore, it is very important to breathe, stretch, and be in a proper state at the time of a presentation. Something incredibly enjoyable is doing grounding exercises. This chapter is just for body and breathing exercises for you to ground.

Alexander Lowen developed these techniques. He is the creator of Bioenergetics, and his work was inspired by William Reich, a follower of Freud who created the theory of armoring, a theory on how we can heal our traumas through our own bodies.

Many times, the person who is a plankton, which does not have a cervical spine, the person who seems to be all bent over, apologizing for existing, is insecure or is just carrying a trauma. I practice bioenergetics, yoga with active meditation, and kundalini.

These are very good exercises that make us stay in the present, here and now, and somehow manage to connect better with our essence, and consequently, with our audience.

Voice modulation

An excellent book that I highly recommend is *The Intelligence of Charisma*, by Heni Ozi Cukier. The author takes a super-scientific approach to how you can develop, in a non-innate way, the science of conquering and influencing people.

He mentions a fact that I find very curious: up to 38% of what I understand from a message is about the tone of voice that is used with me; that is modulation.

In written messages, uppercase letters sound like shouting.

CAN YOU SEE HOW BOTHERING PEOPLE

WHO SPEAK LOUDLY ARE?

Just like people who speak with a high-pitched voice, people who speak with a hoarse voice can be off-putting.

Each of these stimuli generates in us a different perception.

This is not Woodstock-people type of talk, no! It is because the energy with which the vocal cords, physically speaking, resonates in our rib cage, through our body.

That is why there are sounds that you feel in your belly, and others that you feel in your heart.

So, I would say it is very important to control the modulation of your voice.

The lack of pauses and the absence of changes in the tone of the voice also take away some of the excellence of the presentation. As well as saying "Aaaaaaah... Hmmm..." Do not do this!

The message conveyed by this is that your cognitive process is not well-formed, that you do not know what you mean, that you are confused, that your reasoning is not clear. And if it is not clear, it is not coherent.

What do you notice when I say, "Aaaaaaaah"? This is my brain as a machine's processing time. Just do not make that sound.

A deep, gravelly voice conveys effective interest, while a high-pitched voice conveys surprise or skepticism. A louder tone of voice gives the impression that you are arrogant.

The good news is that we can train our vocal frequency level. If it is too sharp, you may be seen as nervous or vulnerable. If it is too deep, it can be an unnecessary display of strength and confidence. On the other hand, it can also be seen simply as sincere and credible.

An exercise I like to do when I talk about the tone of voice is to think about Steve Jobs. Remember him introducing the iPhone or iPod? Remember those iconic presentations?

He spoke in an almost flat, stable modulation. He only placed emphasis when he revealed the product or the product's attributes.

He used to walk across the stage, looked down, looked at the audience, and took breaks, right?

It was a theater. He created momentum.

In a way, what you are going to do up there is almost an act. Prepare your voice for it.

I had a drama teacher who said: "you know that an actor or a presenter is good when you mute your television and can understand what he's talking about. It's someone who articulates his or her mouth and voice so beautifully that you can lip-read him or her".

Hands and lips

Hands say a lot about doing, do they not? I build with my hands, and I create and paint with them.

When I hide my hands in my pocket, I am hiding something. My creative ability? What did I do? Not a good sign. So, be careful not to keep your hands in your pockets during any ceremony or presentation.

Another tip about the hands, besides not leaving them in the pocket, is the crossed arms when you are listening to feedback. This is classic.

Arms open, palms exposed. Never in front of your pelvic region: you are not protecting yourself from anything; you are not a goalkeeper, and you are not going to take a hit. Always around the body, breathing calmly. Not that gasping breath.

And serenity, tranquility.

Avoid grabbing your hair.

Hand on chin conveys suspicion.

Hands over lips, which one should avoid biting, unconsciously sends a message of, "I want to say something, but I'm afraid, I'm hesitating".

My mouth wants to say something, but I do not have the courage. What are you avoiding to say?

Our natural tendency is to mirror body language when we have an affinity towards someone. We start to copy their gestures, behaviors, and even actions; this is called limbic resonance, or even isopraxism.

According to Heni Ozi Cukier's book, *Intelligence of Charisma*, limbic resonance is only possible because of oscillating neurons or mirror neurons. They are the ones that coordinate people physically, regulating how and when their bodies move together.

When two people talk in sync, their movements are synchronized, and that is barely noticeable.

You will notice you start to line up, to blink along. The leg is turned to the same side, the supporting hand is the same; it is a very curious process.

Start paying attention to this, and you will become adept of mirroring.

Anything that generates tension
generates attention.

7- CONDUCTING DTRS WITH STYLE: NONVIOLENT COMMUNICATION

Have you ever heard of nonviolent communication? The first time I heard about this term, created by Marshall Rosenberg, I thought: is there such a thig as a nonviolent communication? Is violent communication one person shouting at another? Not necessarily.

The creation of nonviolent communication was based on effective empathetic communication. It states the importance of determining actions with common values.

It is the famous NVC (nonviolent communication), which proposes a distinction between value judgment observations, between feelings and opinions, between needs (or universal values) of strategies, and, finally, between requests.

NVC posits a continuity between the personal, interpersonal, and social spheres, providing what we call communication in practice, that is, empathizing with your listener.

- The first step is observation, the concrete actions we are observing affect our well-being.
- The second step is feelings, how we feel about what we are observing.
- The third step is needs, the needs that are generating these feelings.
- And the fourth step, but not the least important, are actually the requests, the concrete actions we ask people in order to enrich our lives.

"Wow, what a crazy kumbaya babbling!"

I find nonviolent communication very effective in resolving conflicts.

For example, a narrative of intimidation, an *ad baculum*, as a mother would speak to a child: "It's the millionth time I've seen these dirty socks thrown in the middle of the room. Take them now and put them to wash, otherwise I'll ground you". Latina mothers usually speaks like this (at least mine did, lol).

Who has never gone through this situation? How could we do it using nonviolent communication?

Feeling, need, and request:

"Son, when I see your socks lying there on the living room floor, I feel sad because I need a more organized room to be able to maintain harmony in our house. Can you get your socks and put them to wash, please?"

Which will cause more action?

Instead of saying:

"You're cocky, huh? You never accept an invitation to go to my house for the barbecues I organize"; you can say: "Last year you didn't go to the barbecue at home, we missed you a lot. I hope you can go this year".

You will notice the difference, descriptively, without generalizing.

Another way to approach nonviolent communication is to understand feelings and express them appropriately.

Sometimes we think we are angry and say:

"I was humiliated, I was overwhelmed, I was excluded." This is a narrative that exists only inside our heads. There is no such thing. The only thing that exists are feelings: sad, happy, angry, etc. We must label our feelings the right way.

Self-knowledge allows us to give the right name to what we feel, to express ourselves in a better way. So, instead of saying:

"Wow, I was waiting for your feedback on the report, but since you didn't say anything, I had to send it to the board anyway."

You could say:

"I feel safer when I go through the reports first. It would be important for me if I could analyze them before I forwarded them to the board."

It is that simple.

You should also identify the ability to take responsibility for it:

"You always deliver these activities to me at the last minute. You ruined this project."

Instead, you could say:

"I can't work with deliverables at the last minute, I would like to have at least one day for checking and for final adjustments. Could you guys deliver it to me a day earlier?"

And, finally, clear and specific requests.

Instead of:

"I would like my boss to trust me more."

You could say:

"I would like to have the opportunity to lead the project alone for the first time."

Nonviolent communication is a mark of success in our interpersonal and professional relationships.

PERSUASION

8-PERSUASION AND INFLUENCE ON THE MICROCOSM:

MIRRORING AND RAPPORT IN THE CORPORATE WORLD

In the 1960s, a psychologist named Richard Wiseman conducted a social experiment with waiters. He proposed the following: part of the waiters should repeat the customers' orders and call them by name. The other part would act "normally".

It was basically like when you go to large restaurant chains. There, the service is standardized.

Waiters who repeat customers' names and orders were proven to earn 20% more than those who did not.

This experiment showed something that is already known by science and psychology: we copy the other person to comfort them.

This is what we call mirroring or in an academic way, isopraxism. We have already talked a little bit about this when we talked about body language, but it can also be done through spoken words.

Mirroring, in fact, is a tactic widely used by the FBI in negotiations. They repeat the last five words of the sentences that were said.

Next time you watch *Money Heist*, pay attention to the negotiators. They keep repeating themselves all the time because we like to hear our own beliefs being repeated aloud; we like to hear ourselves and recognize ourselves in each other.

Hearing our name is also very important. It creates bonds without confrontation.

So, call people by name. Did you call to complain about the cable company or the airline ticket? The first thing you can do is call the person by their name.

Always notice the person's name on the badge. You humanize that person; you give that person dignity. It is something that may seem obvious and sensible, but in times of despair many people lose track of notions as simple as names.

"I really want to fly to Los Angeles today, but I know that the flight has an overbooking problem and that, possibly, due to the weather inconvenience, it won't take off until tomorrow morning".

I already anticipate and say the objection that this person would give me.

"Mary, I really wanted to see my mother and I know you must be in a lot of trouble; your day must have been terrible, people here screaming at you, but if by chance you have an opportunity to fit someone into this flight, I would like you to consider my name".

So, right away that person starts to feel welcomed – because that person is being treated with dignity – and becomes motivated to solve your problem.

Humanize people! That is empathy. It is the least we can do, isn't it? No one is obliged to tolerate anyone's rudeness.

Corporate world: ignored emails

How to get a reply?

Who has ever been through this situation: you are in an overactive and reciprocal email exchange, but when it comes to the decisive moments, the recipient stops responding?

Really?! There is nothing worse than that.

Our neurotic behavior is already beginning to conjecture:

"Was that word I used what he didn't like?" or "did they change their minds?" or "they don't want the project anymore?" or "why doesn't anyone answer me?"

And then you send another email and again no reply comes.

The best way to respond to an ignored email is a simple question:

"Hello, [Name] are you going to give up on the project?"

I learned that from Chris Voss in his book "Never Split the Difference." He was the head of FBI negotiations for years.

Straight to the point.

I know this is painful for us who are Latinas/x, who have a more non-confronting raising and culture, who do not want to cause trouble, who do not want to bother... who deal with a Catholic guilt different from that of North American culture.

However, what are the scenarios here?

Option A:

They have given up on the project, and then you would rather know that as soon as possible to get organized and not waste your time or theirs anymore.

Or Option B:

A way for you to alert the person who may be sitting unintentionally on top of your project or simply forgetting to give you an answer. It is an opportunity for you to resume the dialogue and make it happen.

Every time I used this strategy, it worked very well. We just need to have the courage to do so.

How to write a persuasive email

Speaking of emails, it is very important for us to know how to write a persuasive email.

First of all: are you going to talk to someone you do not know? If so, ask an acquaintance to quote you in an introduction. This is triangulation: Ask someone to add you to the conversation; do not ask for an introduction to someone who does not like the person you need to meet. It can be mutual, and then you already carry that other person's ethos with you.

A very important thing is the subject of your email. Can you imagine how many spam emails we receive per day? It is important that you be objective to generate curiosity.

"Jane Doe suggested that we connect". Oh, Jane Doe is an important person, I will pause to read this email. Another title where you can pick up exactly that person's interest: "suggestions for how to sell your online course", for example.

I would certainly open this one, as it is a content that I am interested in consuming.

Second point: cut to the chase.

In the introduction, you have to value each other's time. Those who receive emails every day have little time, so get straight to the point, without getting bogged down.

The content has to add value; almost make an advisory, a sample sale to the person. Your lead, in this case, has to realize that your contact is important, that you have something to add, that you will not take his or her time without giving anything in return.

"Maytê, I saw you launched an online course. It is very attractive! It would be interesting for you to add a share button as it propagates internet content more easily. This will increase its authority, and make you more relevant".

Certainly, I would already see the value in that if it was information I did not know.

From the middle to the end of the introduction you already offer a clear benefit, remembering that this is a more commercial introduction, and you will not close the deal right away.

Then, you say: "I have even better and more interesting tips that can make your course more sellable..." And then I will be tempted, I will think about the benefits.

And, in the end, the efficient call to action: "I thought I'd call you tomorrow for a ten-minute talk on the topic. Thursday at 2 pm or 1 pm? What time is best for you?"

Always offer two options. Because if I give them fifteen options, nobody chooses anything. It's like choosing an ice cream out of 250 flavors. So many options! It's confusing.

I have to give you two options so your brain is then wired to make a decision. A or B? X or Y? Straight to the point. I never say: "Check your schedule... and tell me..." – it's very evasive and abstract.

Invite! Call to action and own it.

Humanize people! That is empathy.
It is the least we can do, isn't it?
No one is obligated to tolerate anyone's rudeness.

Triangulation

It is a very good negotiation and approach strategy that goes along the lines of the seductive narrative.

Triangulation is nothing more than arousing the desire of the other if it proves desirable. The main purpose is to show how you are appreciated by other people.

What you have, what you have to offer, the other may also want.

Have you ever noticed that when you go to the bakery, you always want that last piece of cake? You look at the other one that is whole and reject it thinking it must not be so good?

If it were that good, it would not be whole!

Or when you pass in front of two clubs and see one that has a queue and another that does not. Obviously, you want the one with the queue because the other one must not be that good.

It is the same thing with projects. If everyone wants your project, wants your course, wants your presence... Soon, I will want it, too.

No desire is intrinsic. It is emulated. So, triangulation awakens that. You rely on the endorsement of others to build and emulate the desire for what you have to offer.

What is power? Have you ever thought about that?

Power governs the relationships of our lives.

·

The South Korean philosopher Byung-chul Han has a sentence I think is wonderful when he talks about the logic of power: "The more powerful the power, the more silently it will act. Wherever power needs to show itself, it is because it is already weakened".

Power is invisible. The greatest power is the one that does not need to be shouted aloud.

When you cannot see the bonds of power, it is because dominion has already been established. You are already so manipulated that you do not even notice.

There are three types of power:

Soft Power

Hard Power

Smart Power

Soft power is the power of charisma and attraction. Many social, political, and technological changes, which are imposed by contemporary life, are changing work and social relations.

In this context, charisma is a fundamental key to adapting to the new demands of reality.

Charisma is understood as a soft power. It is not imposing; it is pleasant and convinces the other to like you and be inclined to agree with you.

This is a concept that was disseminated by Joseph Nye, one of the leading thinkers in the field of international relations in politics.

To differentiate things, the power of persuasion, attraction, force, and coercion is what he calls hard power.

As if one were a seduction and the other were an intimidation.

Soft power *versus* hard power

He also describes another type of strategic power: smart power, which is the ability to strategically assess when we should use soft power or hard power considering the objectives involved and even the context.

When you combine soft power with hard power, you gain the ability to articulate a certain end according to your influence and persuasion. Smart power is reading the social, personal, and emotional context to achieve a purpose.

Knowing how to persuade is knowing how to have power and influence.

Everything we have seen here in this book – ethos, pathos, logos, intimidation, seduction, provocation, temptation, all the fallacies, all the readings of psychological profiles – will enable you to influence your microcosm and have an active voice in your relationships, whether personal or professional.

We try something and, if it does not work, we try something else. Always remember to be healthy and responsible, ok?

This power can be used for evil. A person like Hitler, who had charisma as well as soft power and hard power, did not use this knowledge for good.

So, with great power also comes great responsibilities, as I quoted in the very first lines from my dear Ben Parker, Spider-Man's uncle.

I hope you know how to use your new power with conscience.

If you have made it this far in the book, one of the two are true:

Either you are a freak who started at the end or you have read it all.

I hope that, with all the knowledge you have now, you will put these learnings to good use with responsibility and empathy.

Make good use of this toolbox you have gained and use it in your personal and professional relationships to achieve greater leadership, autonomy, influence, decision-making power, and become the protagonist of your life and relationships.

I hope you like them.

Do not shrink yourself to fit in a place
that is not your size.
And, especially, if you see that you are bigger than
that space, go away.

BIBLIOGRAPHY

ARISTÓTELES. *Retórica*. São Paulo: WMF Martins Fontes, 2012.

CÍCERO, Marco Túlio. *Do sumo bem e do sumo*. São Paulo: WMF Martins Fontes, 2020.

CUKIER, Heni Ozi. *A inteligência do carisma: A nova ciência por trás do poder de atrair e influenciar*. São Paulo: Planeta, 2019.

FREUD, Sigmund. *O mal-estar na civilização*. São Paulo: Penguin-Companhia, 2011.

GUNN, Joshua. *Speech Craft*. New York: Bedford/St. Martin's, 2017.

HAN, Byung Chul. *O que é poder*. Petrópolis: Vozes, 2019.

LIPOVESTSKY, Gilles. *A sociedade da sedução: Democracia e narcisismo na hipermodernidade liberal.* Barueri: Manole, 2020. / *Plaire et toucher: Essai sur la societe de seduction*

LOWEN, Alexander. *O corpo em terapia: a abordagem bioenergética.* São Paulo: Summus, 1977.

NYE, Joseph. *The Future of Power: Its Changing Nature and Use in the Twenty-first Century.* New York: Public Affairs, 2011.

REICH, Wilhelm. *Psicologia de massas do fascismo.* São Paulo: Martins Fontes, 2019.

SCHOPENHAUER, Arthur. *Como vencer um debate sem precisar ter razão, Arthur Schopenhauer.* Rio de Janeiro: Topbooks, 2003.

VOSS, Chris. *Never Split The Difference: Negotiating as if Your Life Depended on It.* New York: Conerstone, 2016.

ABOUT THE AUTHOR

Winner of Brazil's *The Apprentice* Special Edition, Maytê Carvalho is a marketeer who has appeared as an entrepreneur on *SharkTank* and is one of Brazil's six great female founders, according to GQ magazine-Conde Nast-.

Built on the years of her experiences, this "handbook" is to be consulted in life before job interviews, presentations, and even debates. Any time the reader's journey requires a moment of self-expression, this book provides the stepping stones to promote personal clarity and power within the speaker. The author gives you the tips and tricks she's used to land her jobs, partnerships, and overall success as a businesswoman.

Carvalho translates Aristotle's Rhetoric content into easy-to-digest information, demystifying the complexity of theory into applicable practicality. *Persuasion: How to Pitch Your Ideas and Own the Room* prepares the reader for challenges in communication and expression within the workplace along with personal relationships.

Maytê Carvalho is a best-selling author, has worked as the Director of Business Strategy at TBWA\Chiat Day Los Angeles, and is currently serving as the Chief Growth & Strategy Officer at Cubo, in New York City.

The privilege of a lifetime is being who you are.

CPSIA information can be obtained
at www.ICGtesting.com
Printed in the USA
BVHW090232011022
648448BV00008B/156

9 781737 278023